CW01177528

Original title:
The Distant Gate

Copyright © 2024 Creative Arts Management OÜ
All rights reserved.

Author: Charles Whitfield
ISBN HARDBACK: 978-9916-90-054-3
ISBN PAPERBACK: 978-9916-90-055-0

Beyond the Realm of Now

Time drifts softly, lost in haze,
Whispers linger, fading days.
Hearts unbound, free from chains,
In the silence, hope remains.

Colors dance in twilight's grasp,
Moments fleeting, dreams unmasked.
Beyond the stars, our spirits roam,
In the night, we find our home.

Paths We Never Tread

Footsteps echo on empty roads,
Stories whispered, wisdom loathed.
Choices made, yet paths forgot,
In the shadows, dreams begot.

Lost in time, roads intertwine,
What could be? A fleeting sign.
Memories linger, bittersweet,
On paths we never dare to meet.

Wishing on a Fading Comet

Stars align in cosmic flight,
Wishes whispered into night.
Comets blaze with tales untold,
Burning bright, then turning cold.

In the sky, we aim our dreams,
Fleeting light, or so it seems.
Hold tight to hopes that softly gleam,
Life's a dance, a tender dream.

The Bridge of Forgotten Dreams

Over waters, shadows cast,
Whispers of a broken past.
Step by step, the bridge will sway,
Carrying thoughts that drift away.

Memories fade like evening mist,
Promises lost, moments missed.
Yet hope lingers, softly beams,
On this bridge of forgotten dreams.

A Riddle Written in the Sky

Clouds weave tales in the blue,
Whispers dance in the air,
Shadows chase the sunlight,
Secrets linger everywhere.

Stars blink like knowing eyes,
Moonlight spills on the sea,
Galaxies spin their stories,
Cosmic paths set us free.

Dragonflies flit in twilight,
Sketching dreams by the pond,
Nature scribbles in silence,
An enigma to respond.

Hearts ponder the vast unknown,
Questions drift with the breeze,
In the riddle of the sky,
Find the truth that brings peace.

When Distance Breathes

Whispering winds carry sighs,
Feelings stretch like the sea,
Time folds like an old book,
In pages where we used to be.

Mountains stand between us,
Yet, they cannot dim the flame,
Every heartbeat echoes softly,
Distance whispers your name.

Stars pull at my heartstrings,
Painted across the dark night,
I send my love in a letter,
On wings of silver light.

Connection lies in the space,
Where silence knows our song,
Even when distance breathes,
In our hearts, we belong.

The Journey of an Ever-Searching Heart

Paths winding through the forest,
Footsteps write a tale anew,
Every turn brings new colors,
In the canvas of the view.

Mountains rise like old friends,
Tempting the daring soul,
With each challenge faced, we grow,
Each victory makes us whole.

Stream's song dances around us,
Guiding with gentle grace,
In the depths of every journey,
Find the strength to embrace.

Through valleys of shadow and light,
Seeking warmth in the cold,
An ever-searching heart wanders,
With dreams that never grow old.

A Portal to Time's Embrace

In the hush of night, whispers flow,
A doorway glimmers, soft and low.
Ancient shadows dance in tune,
Eyes reflect the silver moon.

Through the veil, stories unfold,
Fragments of the brave and bold.
Time's embrace, a gentle kiss,
Moments linger, dreamer's bliss.

Secrets in the Twilight Veil

Beneath the stars, where silence sings,
Hidden truths take silent wings.
In twilight's grasp, the world slows,
Mysteries in the night wind blows.

Echoes of laughter softly fade,
In the shadows, memories played.
A tapestry of dusk and dawn,
Secrets weave, forever drawn.

The Wandering Light

A flicker here, a shimmer there,
Guiding souls with gentle care.
Through darkened paths, it leads the way,
Awakens dreams that silently lay.

The wandering light, it knows no bounds,
In every heart, its warmth resounds.
A beacon bright in endless night,
Unveiling hope, inflaming sight.

Gates of Memory's Passage

Rusty hinges cry in sighs,
Open gates to past replies.
Visions dance in a faded breeze,
Time stands still as hearts find ease.

Each step echoes with a story,
Moments lost in faded glory.
In the corridor's soft embrace,
Memory's touch, a sacred space.

Sentries of the Starry Abyss

Guardians of the night sky,
Whispers of cosmic dreams,
They watch with ancient eyes,
Through the dark, the starlight beams.

On the edge of endless void,
Where time forgets to race,
Each flicker bears a story,
Of a distant, timeless place.

Guiding souls who wander,
In search of a shining path,
Sentries keep their vigil,
In the universe's warm hearth.

Beneath the sea of silence,
Curiosity ignites,
As we reach for their secrets,
In the canvas of the nights.

The Unseen Threshold

Veils of mystery surround,
Whispers linger in the air,
Each step leads to unknown,
A world beyond compare.

Footfalls soft on dusty ground,
Echoes cross the divide,
A beckoning sensation,
Where dreams and truths collide.

Eyes peer through the curtain,
Of shimmered, hazy light,
A glimpse of what could be,
In the soft, deep twilight.

In the silence of the moment,
The heart begins to race,
Along this unseen threshold,
We seek our rightful place.

Through the Lattice of Lost Time

Memories weave like shadows,
Entangled in the past,
Through the lattice of lost time,
We find the spells that last.

Fleeting glimpses in the dark,
Flicker like a flame,
Each thread pulls at our hearts,
Calling out our names.

Hours dance like fireflies,
In a night sky surreal,
We unravel their stories,
Feeling what they reveal.

In every winding passage,
Secrets wait to be found,
Through the lattice of lost time,
We reclaim our ground.

Portals to Unsung Places

Whispers dwell in hidden nooks,
Behind a silver door,
Portals calling to our minds,
To riches made of lore.

Each fold in space a promise,
Of realms yet unexplored,
Adventures crawl along the seams,
Of dreams we can afford.

In shadows thick with silence,
We step with bated breath,
Into the tapestry of time,
Defying fear and death.

With every threshold crossed anew,
Secrets bid us chase,
Portals to unsung places,
Woven in a boundless grace.

Tales From the Outer Lands

In the lands where whispers roam,
   Secrets buried far from home.
  Stars align in evening's glow,
   Echoes of the tales we know.

Mountains high and valleys low,
  Beyond the rivers' steady flow.
  Ancient trees, their stories tell,
Of magic realms where dreamers dwell.

Through the mist, a figure glides,
With every step, the mystery hides.
  Crafting paths of twilight shade,
   In the silence, legends made.

Lost in time, the voices sing,
Of daring hearts and the hope they bring.
  In every stone, a story lies,
  From outer lands beneath the skies.

Fading Footprints in the Twilight

As day departs and shadows creep,
Footprints fade in silence deep.
Whispers linger on the breeze,
Telling tales of love and ease.

A fading light, the stars ignite,
Guiding souls through the encroaching night.
In twilight's grasp, we find our way,
Chasing dreams that drift and sway.

With every step, the world grows dim,
The echoes of a life on whim.
And as we walk this path alone,
The twilight sings, our thoughts as stone.

But in the dusk, hope holds its ground,
In fading footprints, love is found.
Through every heart, the stories flow,
In twilight's arms, we learn to grow.

Ethereal Roads of Silent Dreams

Beneath the moon's soft, silver beams,
Lie the ethereal roads of dreams.
Where shadows dance and whispers play,
In silent realms where phantoms sway.

A journey taken, hearts entwined,
In twilight's glow, our fates aligned.
Through corridors of time we roam,
In search of love, a place called home.

The stars above weave tales in light,
Guiding us through the endless night.
Each step we take, the world transforms,
Into a canvas where hope conforms.

On roads of whispers, we shall soar,
In silent dreams, forevermore.
Bound by the magic, intertwined,
Ethereal roads, where souls unwind.

Chasing Shadows of Yesterday

In the corners where memories play,
We find ourselves in shades of gray.
Chasing shadows lost in time,
Echoes fading, a distant rhyme.

Through the alleys of our past,
Fleeting moments fade too fast.
Each heartbeat whispers, softly calls,
Woven paths where longing sprawls.

But shadows cling like morning mist,
Reminding us of what we've missed.
Yet in their depths, a light remains,
A spark ignites amidst our pains.

So let us chase, for in the flight,
We find the strength to seek the light.
In yesterday's arms, we learn and grow,
Chasing shadows, we find our glow.

Chasing Shadows in Twilight

In twilight's glow, shadows dance,
Whispers of dreams in fleeting chance.
The world dims low, colors blend,
As night descends, our thoughts extend.

Footsteps soft on the muted ground,
Echoes of laughter, a joyful sound.
Stars awaken, the night unfolds,
Each secret lost, each story told.

Silhouettes sway beneath the moon,
As time drifts by, a gentle tune.
In the chill, hearts beat as one,
Chasing shadows 'til night is done.

With every step, a path is traced,
In twilight's arms, our fears erased.
Through the dark, we seek the light,
Chasing shadows, we reunite.

The Compass of Reading Stars

Beneath the vast and endless night,
Stars become our guiding light.
Each twinkle tells a tale so old,
A compass for the brave and bold.

Through constellations, hearts can steer,
Mapping dreams with hope and cheer.
A journey starts with every glance,
Reading stars, we take a chance.

Galaxies whisper secrets deep,
In their embrace, our souls do leap.
With every wish upon a spark,
We navigate the endless dark.

The cosmos sings a song of peace,
In every heartbeat, we find release.
With starlit paths, we chart our way,
The compass of dreams will guide our stay.

Beneath the Surface of the Known

Beneath the waves, secrets lie,
Waiting still, a soft goodbye.
Dark waters hide what we can't see,
In depths unknown, we yearn to be.

Past the shore, where shadows creep,
Whispers linger in silence deep.
Each ripple tells a story faint,
Of hopes and fears we dare to paint.

Exploring realms where light is scarce,
We dive into a world of chance.
Through the murk, our hearts will flow,
Beneath the surface, truth will grow.

In twilight depths, we seek to find,
The hidden gems of the heart and mind.
With courage, we will learn to see,
Beneath the surface, we are free.

Embracing the Enigma of Distance

Distance weaves a complex thread,
Connecting hearts, though far we tread.
In every mile, a story spins,
Of loves and losses, hopes that win.

Through valleys low and mountains high,
Our spirit soars, it yearns to fly.
In fragile bonds, we trust the roam,
Embracing distance, we find home.

The space between is not a wall,
But echoes of laughter, a tender call.
Each heartbeat travels through the air,
As whispers dance, we're always there.

Though miles may stand like oceans wide,
Love's gentle touch will be our guide.
In every moment, we will know,
Embracing distance, hearts will glow.

A Symphony of Uncharted Paths

The road ahead is wild and free,
Where shadows dance beneath the trees.
Each step a note in nature's song,
An echo where the dreams belong.

With every turn, a story waits,
A rhythm weaves through twisting fates.
The heart beats loud, the spirit flies,
A symphony beneath the skies.

Whispers in the Twilight Fog

In twilight's hush, the whispers call,
With secrets soft that gently fall.
The fog wraps round like a silken shroud,
Where thoughts arise, both clear and loud.

Through misty nights, the dreams unfold,
In shadows, tales are softly told.
The world, it breathes a ghostly air,
With every step, a hidden prayer.

The Lament of the Wanderer

A road untraveled, alone I tread,
With memories kept of paths I fled.
The stars above, they guide my tears,
A song of loss through endless years.

Each mile a weight upon my soul,
Searching for solace, a distant goal.
The wind it sighs of burdens borne,
In silence deep, I am reborn.

Journeying Through the Unknown Midnight

In midnight's cloak, I wander far,
With only dreams to be my star.
Each shadow holds a fleeting light,
A beacon bright in endless night.

With every step, the courage grows,
Through silent paths where mystery flows.
The heart, it leaps with every sound,
For in the dark, my soul is found.

A Murmur from the Beyond

Whispers dance in twilight's glow,
Echoes from the depths below.
Ghostly tales of dreams unspun,
Linger soft as day is done.

A sigh of stars in night's embrace,
Threads of time in quiet space.
Secrets shared with passing breeze,
Carried forth through ancient trees.

Ethereal songs of yore,
Fill the air forevermore.
With every heartbeat, shadows play,
In the dim light, fade away.

Crossing the Divide of Imagined Places

Bridges built from thoughts and dreams,
Flowing like soft, whispering streams.
Step beyond the edge of thought,
Find the worlds that time forgot.

Mountains rise from vivid hue,
Skies of pink where hopes renew.
With each step, the mind expands,
Crafting visions from gentle hands.

Between the lines of stories told,
Lies the magic, brave and bold.
Crossing realms where shadows dwell,
In the silence, all is well.

The Color of Distant Light

Fleeting rays from far-off stars,
Paint the night with glowing scars.
In the deep, a shimmer grows,
A cascade of dreams that flows.

Crimson whispers, emerald gleams,
Caught in the net of silent dreams.
Colors blend where lost souls roam,
In the ether, they find home.

Each hue a story waiting there,
In the silence, love and care.
Kindred spirits touch the night,
With hearts aglow in distant light.

Beyond Sand and Sea

Where the horizon meets the sky,
Waves of sand and whispers sigh.
Footprints left on golden shores,
Memories linger, hearts explore.

Salt and sun weave tales so grand,
Time conspired as we stand.
Together lost in nature's song,
A bond that feels forever strong.

Beyond the tides, a dream unfolds,
In the warmth, a future holds.
Hand in hand with each new dawn,
In a world where love goes on.

The Silence of Open Doors

In the hush of twilight's glow,
Whispers linger, soft and low.
Promises lie in shadows cast,
Memories of a fleeting past.

Each door waits with breath held tight,
Guarding secrets from the light.
Paths untaken, dreams held dear,
In silence, all we want is near.

The air is thick with what might be,
Echoes fade into the sea.
Lost in thought, we stand and stare,
The open doors, a silent prayer.

In the stillness, hearts will mend,
As these open spaces lend,
Hope and longing, side by side,
In the silence, we confide.

Footsteps on Distant Shores

Footprints mark the sandy clay,
Carried by the tide's ballet.
Echoes of the past resound,
In the wind, lost dreams are found.

Seagulls cry in the morning air,
Salt and sun, a lover's care.
Each step whispers tales untold,
Of adventures brave and bold.

Waves that fiercely kiss the land,
Draw us close, then slip like sand.
In each ripple, stories dance,
Inviting hearts to take a chance.

Footsteps fading, leaving traces,
On these shores, time's wild embraces.
Every path a journey's lore,
Onward still, to distant shores.

A Gateway of Stars Above

A canvas painted deep and wide,
Where countless dreams and wishes hide.
Stars like jewels spark and gleam,
In the night, a quiet dream.

Galaxies swirl in a timeless dance,
Inviting all to take a chance.
With every twinkle, hopes ignite,
And guide us through the endless night.

Mysteries beckon, call us near,
Navigating with hearts sincere.
Each brilliant point, a guiding light,
A gateway bright in the velvet night.

As we gaze at the cosmos vast,
Moments linger, shadows cast.
In this wonder, fears dissolve,
A gateway of stars to resolve.

The Winding Road to Elsewhere

Curves and bends that lead the way,
Unseen paths where spirits play.
Each turn a tale yet to be,
A journey crafted endlessly.

Through forests thick and valleys deep,
Secrets hidden that we keep.
Mountains tall that touch the sky,
In their shadow, dreams can fly.

With every mile, the heart feels free,
Inviting winds whisper of glee.
The road unfolds like a sweet embrace,
Leading us to a better place.

So wander on, through dark and light,
Embrace the day, cherish the night.
For on this road, we find our theme,
The winding path to every dream.

Whispers Beyond the Horizon

Softly the sun dips low,
Painting the sky in gold.
Waves whisper secrets sweet,
Of stories yet untold.

Glimmers dance on the sea,
As night begins to fall.
Stars spark in the velvet,
A celestial call.

Dreams take flight on the breeze,
Carried far and wide.
In the hush of twilight,
Hope does not subside.

Listen to the silence,
Let your heart embrace.
Whispers of the future,
In this tranquil space.

Shadows of the Forgotten Path

Winding through the twisted trees,
Shadows softly creep.
Echoes of the past linger,
In the silence deep.

Footsteps fade on dusty trails,
Where stories long reside.
Ancient whispers call to me,
From the time they hide.

Moonlight drapes a silver veil,
On a world left behind.
Searching for those fleeting dreams,
That the night has dined.

In this maze of memories,
I wander and I seek.
Shadows of the forgotten,
Breathe, but do not speak.

Echoes of an Unseen Journey

A road that winds and bends,
Veiled in morning mist.
Whispers of what might have been,
In the silence kissed.

Footfalls light as fleeting hearts,
Trace the dreams we chase.
Through the echoes of our hopes,
We find our rightful place.

Waves of time wash over us,
Memories ebb and flow.
In the stillness of the hour,
We nurture what we know.

Each step is but a promise,
A bloom upon the way.
Echoes of an unseen road,
Guide us through the day.

Beyond the Faraway Threshold

A door ajar, a welcoming light,
Holds the promise of grace.
Beyond the faraway threshold,
A new world to embrace.

Whispers from the unknown call,
With each soft, beckoning sigh.
Adventure waits in secret places,
As the moments fly.

With courage born of wanderlust,
I step into the bright.
Beyond the faraway threshold,
Hope ignites the night.

As shadows fall behind me now,
The future starts to gleam.
In this realm of endless wonder,
I dare to dream my dream.

The Unseen Gatekeeper's Tale

In twilight's embrace, the shadows creep,
A watcher stands where secrets sleep.
With breath held close, the world unfolds,
The gatekeeper's tale in whispers told.

Veils of silence drape the night,
Stars unveil their hidden light.
Each moment lingers in soft breath,
A dance between life and death.

Paths converge where time stands still,
He guides the lost, the dreams fulfill.
An unseen force with gentle hands,
Nurturing hope, as destiny stands.

Through silence deep and shadows wide,
In his realm, the brave confide.
The gatekeeper's heart beats pure and strong,
In the echoes, we find where we belong.

Reflections of the Boundless Journey.

In every step, a story spun,
Across the land beneath the sun.
Mountains high and valleys low,
In every heart, the wanderlust flows.

The rivers sing of dreams once sought,
In ripples cast, lessons taught.
Memories dance upon the breeze,
Whispers of old adventures tease.

Each horizon brings a new delight,
Stars awaken in the night.
With eyes wide open, paths will weave,
In the journey's heart, our souls believe.

Time stretches like the endless sea,
Where all that was, and all will be.
In the tapestry of dusk and dawn,
The boundless voyage carries on.

Whispers Beyond the Horizon

In the distance, echoes call,
Whispers dancing, near and small.
Beyond the hills where shadows play,
A promise made at break of day.

The clouds drift past, a fleeting song,
Each note a wish where dreams belong.
Footsteps light on paths unknown,
Through twilight's glow, the seeds are sown.

In the silence, messages ride,
Carried forth on the evening tide.
Voices weave in gentle sighs,
The horizon beckons, where hope flies.

Look beyond to what may be,
A world of wonder waits to see.
In whispers soft, the future gleams,
Beyond the horizon, we chase our dreams.

Shadows of an Untold Journey

Beneath the moon, the shadows swirl,
A tapestry of dreams unfurl.
Each step whispers secrets deep,
Of journeys taken, sowed not cheap.

Through tangled woods and silent glades,
The heart seeks truth where light invades.
With every turn, a tale begins,
In the echoes of where it spins.

Misty veils hide stories vast,
Of moments lost and futures cast.
In every shadow lies a spark,
Guiding lost souls through the dark.

Untamed paths call the brave in heart,
To find the light, the light of art.
Through shadows deep, we find the way,
To rise anew with each new day.

Fading Footprints on Foreign Soil

Steps whisper tales of the past,
Lost in the shadows, fading fast.
Each grain of sand tells a story,
Of travelers seeking fleeting glory.

Winds carry remnants of dreams,
Echoes of laughter, silent screams.
Footprints washed by the rising tide,
In this vast land, no place to hide.

Mountains loom, their peaks untouched,
Beneath their weight, hearts are clutched.
In foreign soil, we search for home,
Yet wanderers never face the loam.

A path less taken leads us on,
In the dusk where hope has drawn.
As shadows blend with departing light,
We chase the dusk into the night.

The Land of Unseen Dreams

In the shroud of night, dreams arise,
Whispers of truths in the starlit skies.
Beyond the veil of waking light,
The land of unseen waits, inviting sight.

Here, wishes take flight on paper wings,
Unruly and wild, like forgotten kings.
Each shadow dances, a curious spark,
Illuminating paths through the dark.

In this realm where silence reigns,
Unspoken longing threads the chains.
Hearts entwined in an ethereal weave,
Where hope is nurtured, and souls believe.

The canvas stretches, vast and wide,
With colors whispered by the tide.
In dreams we wander, forever free,
In the land of unseen, just you and me.

Far Beyond the Common Horizon

Past the hills where the sun dips low,
Lies a world few ever know.
Waves of wonder beckon us forth,
To the edges of our own rebirth.

Skies painted bright with tales untold,
In every heartbeat, adventures bold.
Clouds drift by like cotton dreams,
Whispering secrets in silver streams.

Mountains rise where eagles soar,
In their shadow, we long for more.
Yet the horizon, a distant line,
Calls us onward to explore, divine.

The journey unfolds, a tapestry wide,
With every step, our fears collide.
In the twilight's glow, we find our place,
Far beyond the horizon's embrace.

A Kaleidoscope of Untraveled Paths

A prism of choices, bright and vast,
Each turn a memory, a shadow cast.
Winding through dreams, we wander free,
In a kaleidoscope of what could be.

Colors blend in the morning light,
Every path holds a new delight.
Echoes linger where footsteps fall,
Tales intertwine, binding us all.

The journey is painted with threads of gold,
A tapestry woven, stories told.
As we explore this vibrant expanse,
We find our rhythm, join in the dance.

In every twist, a chance to grow,
In the heart's quiet, a wisdom flows.
A kaleidoscope turning, ever alive,
In the untraveled paths, we thrive.

Fantasies Knotted in the Weavings of Time

In twilight's glow, dreams intertwine,
Threads of fate, dancing on the line.
Whispers of old, in shadows cast,
Echoes linger, binding the past.

Moments weave, a tapestry grand,
Each fleeting sigh, a soft command.
Memories bloom like flowers in spring,
Holding the secrets that shadows sing.

In the loom of night, stars align,
Crafting tales that age cannot confine.
Fantasies flourish in the mind's domain,
Timeless stories etched in life's grain.

Embrace the journey, hearts set free,
In every knot, a mystery.
Time's gentle fingers, working the rhyme,
We find our truths in the weavings of time.

The Traveler's Silent Yearnings

A distant horizon calls my name,
Waves of wonder, igniting the flame.
Footsteps echo on roads unknown,
In silent dreams, seeds of hope are sown.

Each sunrise paints the path anew,
Whispers of places waiting too.
Mountains rise like guardians bold,
In tales of journeys, stories unfold.

Lonely paths under a silver sky,
Emotions linger as starlings fly.
Every mile, a story untold,
In the traveler's heart, treasures of gold.

Though silence follows, the spirit roams,
In every step, discovery homes.
With open roads like a canvas wide,
Yearnings whisper in the wanderer's stride.

Vistas of an Enchanted Tomorrow

Beyond the hills, where dreams take flight,
Awaits a dawn bathed in golden light.
Each moment dances in soft embrace,
Painting visions of a hopeful place.

Rivers flow with laughter and song,
Nature's embrace, where we belong.
Every leaf tells stories of old,
Vistas unfolding, vibrant and bold.

In the whispering winds, futures bloom,
The scent of magic fills the room.
Tomorrow beckons with arms so wide,
In its promise, we shall confide.

Through every trial, beauty we find,
In the boundless heart of humankind.
Embrace the dawn, let worries cease,
For enchanted tomorrows promise peace.

Echoes of an Ancient Voyage

Sails unfurl 'neath the starlit skies,
An ancient tale where the spirit flies.
Waves carry whispers of ages past,
In the heart of the ocean, memories last.

The compass spins, guiding the way,
Through tempests fierce and gentle sway.
Chasing the horizon, stars in sight,
An echo of journeys in the night.

With each surge, the stories flow,
Tales of sailors, brave and slow.
Voices of old in the salty air,
A fusion of wisdom, lost in despair.

The sea remembers every song sung,
In the depths, the ancient is young.
Echoes resonate, the voyage calls,
In the heart of the sailor, adventure enthralls.

Echoing Dreams from the Abyss

In shadows deep where silence dwells,
A whisper calls from hidden wells.
The echoes dance like fleeting light,
In dreams that drift beyond the night.

Amidst the depths where secrets rest,
Yearnings pulse within the chest.
A haunting song, a siren's plea,
Draws souls to realms of mystery.

With every tide, the heartbeats blend,
In liquid fate, they twist and bend.
The abyss holds tales yet untold,
As secrets of the night unfold.

Awake, and let the dreams ignite,
Through tangled fears, embrace the light.
For in the depths where shadows play,
A journey waits to guide the way.

The Horizon's Unfolding Mystery

Beneath the sky, where colors blend,
The horizon whispers, curves and bends.
Each dawn a canvas, fresh and bright,
Unfolding secrets made of light.

With every wave that greets the shore,
A tale of wonder to explore.
The sun ascends, a golden flame,
Lighting paths we cannot name.

Clouds dance softly in the breeze,
In silence, hold our heart's unease.
Yet hope lingers with each new day,
Guiding dreams along the way.

Embrace the journey, lost and found,
In every step, let joy abound.
For mysteries await the bold,
In horizons vast, their stories told.

Gazing Upon the Untouched Horizon

A canvas stretched, in hues so rare,
The untouched horizon calls to dare.
With every glance, a heart might soar,
To places dreamed of, evermore.

The sun dips low, a warm embrace,
Illuminating time and space.
With whispered winds that gently tease,
The horizon breathes, a tranquil breeze.

Each star that twinkles in the night,
A glimmer of hope, a spark of light.
Forever constant through the years,
Reflecting dreams and hidden fears.

So gaze upon that distant line,
Where earth and sky in shadows twine.
For in that space, the soul will find,
A world of wonders yet undefined.

Pathways Illuminated by Stars

Through velvet skies where starlight sweeps,
Life's winding paths in silence peeps.
Each step adorned by cosmic glow,
Guiding hearts where few may go.

With every twinkle comes a tale,
Of journeys bold and dreams not frail.
The constellations sing in time,
A melody, a rhythm, a rhyme.

These pathways stretch beyond the night,
Embraced by warmth, enveloped in light.
Each footfall whispers secrets old,
Of stories lost and passions bold.

So tread with hope through starlit lands,
For destiny lies in unseen hands.
In every turn, let wonder steer,
As pathways shine and skies draw near.

A Journey to the Other Side

Through silver mist the shadows glide,
Whispers of dreams, a gentle tide.
Each step forward, a heartbeats' call,
Fading echoes, we rise or fall.

With every breath, the world expands,
We trace the lines with hopeful hands.
Stars above, our guiding fire,
In the unknown, we dare aspire.

Moments linger, time stands still,
Chasing wishes beyond the hill.
Onward we move, with faith as guide,
Unlocking doors to the other side.

The Enigma of Dusk and Dawn

Twilight dances with fading light,
A soft embrace of day and night.
Shadows whisper secrets untold,
In the silence, mysteries unfold.

Golden hues kissed by the stars,
Dreams awaken, breaking bars.
Each face of time wears a unique mask,
In the space between, we dare to ask.

A canvas stretched with hues divine,
The brush of fate, our hearts align.
Between dusk's sigh and dawn's sweet breath,
Lies the riddle that defies death.

Portraits of Untraveled Dreams

In stillness waits a painted scene,
A world unknown, serene, unseen.
Each stroke reveals a hidden light,
A glimpse of hope amidst the night.

Fingers sketch what hearts can't say,
Visions dance in shades of gray.
Across the canvas, whispers play,
Silent stories yearning to stay.

With every line, a journey starts,
Mapping dreams within our hearts.
Untraveled paths, adventures call,
In portraits drawn, we find our all.

The Light at the Edge of Infinity

At the horizon where whispers fade,
A spark ignites, a timeless cascade.
Beyond the void, where moments blend,
Lies a promise that shall not end.

Shadows stretch, the night draws near,
But in the dark, a vision clear.
The light, a beacon, guiding forth,
Illuminating our true worth.

Crossing thresholds, we seek to find,
The brilliance born from the blind.
At the edge where dreams collide,
We embrace the light, forever tied.

A Map in the Heart of Solitude

In silence deep, a dream takes flight,
A path unseen, both strange and bright.
Lost in thought, the heart will roam,
Drawing maps to find a home.

Where shadows dance and whispers flow,
The compass points to what we know.
Each heartbeat marks a step anew,
In solitude, the soul breaks through.

With ink of night on paper white,
The lines will guide through edge of light.
Though winds may howl and storms may form,
The inner peace will keep us warm.

So take a breath, embrace the still,
The heart's own map shall bend to will.
Through quiet paths, the spirit's art,
Find the treasure in the heart.

Beyond the Borders of Perception

In realms unseen where shadows play,
The mind expands, then slips away.
Thoughts wander past the common thread,
To mysteries where dreams are fed.

Colors blend in shifting skies,
A world reborn when vision lies.
The light unveils what's left unspoke,
In echoes soft, reality broke.

A tapestry of hopes entwined,
In whispers, truths we long to find.
Through every twist, each turn anew,
Perception shifts, revealing hue.

So dare to see beyond the veil,
Where timid hearts may oft turn pale.
In endless quests, the seekers seek,
A wisdom found in silence deep.

The Lighthouse of the Lost

Amidst the fog, a beacon shines,
A guiding light through tangled pines.
For those adrift on seas so wide,
A refuge waits where souls might bide.

With steady flame, it calls the way,
To navigate the stormy gray.
In shadows deep, lost hearts can rest,
Embraced within its glowing chest.

The waves may crash, the winds may wail,
Yet still, the light will not grow pale.
For every ship that seeks the shore,
The lighthouse stands, forevermore.

In darkest nights, it whispers hope,
To guide the weary, help them cope.
So let the light, through trials tossed,
Be the home of every lost.

Fables from Far-Off Lands

Once upon a time, tales unfurled,
Of distant realms and a wondrous world.
With every turn, a lesson learned,
As fires blazed, and hearts burned.

From mountains high to valleys low,
Each story rich with wisdom's glow.
The stars would dance in youthful glee,
For every fable held a key.

Through tangled woods and rivers vast,
Heroes rise from shadows cast.
In ancient tongues, the truth unfolds,
In every tale, a treasure holds.

So gather 'round, let voices blend,
As tales of old become our friends.
In fables told by ages passed,
The spirit lives, forever lasts.

The Stargazer's Silent Wish

Under the night sky, stars brightly gleam,
A starlit whisper, a fading dream.
Hands clasped in prayer, hope takes its flight,
In silence, the heart speaks to the night.

Each twinkling light, a story untold,
Wishes entwined in the cosmos bold.
The universe listens, a vast embrace,
In the stillness, finds its sacred space.

With every glance, the soul starts to soar,
A journey of wonder, forevermore.
In galaxies far, where the brave souls roam,
The stargazer wishes to find their home.

A silent vow beneath the moon's gaze,
In the heart of the cosmos, lost in a maze.
Hope drifts softly on celestial streams,
Awaiting the dawn of forgotten dreams.

Fantasies Across the Divide

In realms of shadow, where dreams collide,
Whispers of hope in the fading tide.
Visions of warmth, where the heart can mend,
Fantasies linger, a lover's transcend.

Across the divide, mere miles apart,
Yet close in the echoes of every heart.
A tapestry woven of longing and grace,
In the silence, we find our own place.

Time weaves our spirits with threads of light,
Crafting connections that feel so right.
In moments of stillness, our dreams intertwine,
Fantasies cherished, forever we'll shine.

Though distances stretch like a vast ocean,
Love fuels the fire, a heartfelt devotion.
Together we'll wander, hand in hand,
Through fantasies born of a timeless land.

The Allure of the Unreachable

In the horizon where the sky kisses land,
Lies the allure that we cannot command.
A mountain so high, kissed by the sun,
Its peak calls the dreamers, the brave and the fun.

Like stars in the sky, just out of reach,
Lessons in longing, the universe teaches.
To chase the impossible, to fight the good fight,
To dance with the shadows and embrace the light.

Winds carry whispers of unclaimed desire,
Fueling our passion, igniting the fire.
In every heartbeat, a story unfolds,
The unreachable dreams, daring and bold.

We climb and we stumble, but never give in,
For in the pursuit, our true lives begin.
With skies as our canvas and dreams as our guide,
We chase the allure of the unreachable wide.

Pages of a Journey Yet to Be

Ink flows like rivers on blank, waiting sheets,
Each word a step where the heart gently meets.
Stories uncharted lie deep in the mind,
Pages of a journey, waiting to find.

With every new chapter, the past drifts away,
A tapestry woven, a new dawn's play.
In whispers of hope, our futures we trace,
Turning the pages of time and of space.

The quill dances softly, each stroke a new start,
Crafting the stories that flow from the heart.
In the margins, the laughter, the tears that we keep,
Pages of a journey, where memories sleep.

So turn every leaf, let the adventure unfold,
In unspoken dreams, let our lives be told.
For journeys await in the tales that we weave,
Pages of a journey, together we'll leave.

Dreams of a Secluded Realm

In the twilight, shadows play,
Whispers of the night decay.
Through the leaves, a soft caress,
In this world, I find my rest.

Beneath the stars, a hidden glow,
Where silent winds of secrets flow.
Time stands still, a gentle balm,
In this dream, I feel so calm.

Rivers twist through ancient trees,
Carrying tales on the breeze.
Here, the heart finds its lost creed,
In solitude, I am freed.

Veils of mist, a soft embrace,
Memories linger, leaving trace.
In the quiet, magic swells,
In this realm, my spirit dwells.

The Bridge to Lost Horizons

Across the vale where shadows creep,
A bridge appears, the secrets keep.
With every step, the past awakes,
A path where destiny remakes.

Oh, distant shores, I seek your light,
In twilight's glow, a guiding sight.
Echoes of laughter, whispers low,
Through the mist, the memories flow.

Fate's gentle hand transforms the air,
Weaving dreams with tender care.
Onward I journey, heart in hand,
To that far-off, forgotten land.

Each heartbeat thrums with ancient song,
In the night, where I belong.
A bridge unites the near and far,
To lost horizons, my guiding star.

Liminal Spaces and Silent Promises

In twilight hours, where dreams align,
Liminal spaces, threads entwine.
A pause between the now and then,
In silence, whispers stir again.

Boundaries blur, the shadows rise,
A dance of echoes, soft goodbyes.
Each step a memory, more profound,
In the stillness, magic found.

Promises linger on the breeze,
Carrying hopes like falling leaves.
In moments fleeting, time is steep,
Within these realms, our secrets keep.

With every breath, a fleeting spark,
Guides the way through shadows dark.
In the hush, our voices blend,
In this space, our hearts transcend.

Chasing Sparks of Distant Stars

A canvas black, with twinkling lights,
Chasing dreams on starry nights.
From earth we gaze at heights unknown,
Yearning for worlds we've never grown.

Galaxies whisper tales of old,
Of journeys taken, brave and bold.
With every wish upon a spark,
We chase the light, igniting dark.

In the cosmos, wide and grand,
Our spirits soar, hand in hand.
Stardust trails in endless flight,
Through distant realms, we seek the light.

With hearts ablaze, we navigate,
To find the worlds that wait our fate.
Each spark a tale, a hope anew,
In the night sky, dreams come true.

Echoes from the Faraway

Whispers from the distant shore,
Carrying tales of days of yore.
Each wave a song, each breeze a sigh,
Echoes linger as time drifts by.

Stars alight in velvet skies,
Glimmers of hopes, where silence lies.
Memories dance on the moonlit sea,
Calling the hearts that long to be free.

Ancient stones hold secrets old,
In their grip, the stories unfold.
Step softly where shadows play,
Feel the echoes, come what may.

The horizon beckons, a distant call,
To those who wander, to those who fall.
In the stillness, hear the lore,
Of echoes from the evermore.

When Dreams Kiss the Twilight

In twilight's glow, the dreams take flight,
Soft whispers weave in the fading light.
Stars awaken to a gentle tune,
As night embraces the silver moon.

Colors blend in a soft embrace,
Casting shadows, painting grace.
Visions swirl like a gentle breeze,
Carrying hopes through the ancient trees.

Time slows down in this sacred hour,
Where wishes bloom like a midnight flower.
Heartbeats sync with the night's sweet breath,
In moments born from life and death.

As dreams unfold in the still of dusk,
The world transforms in a fragrant musk.
Two souls collide, as stars align,
In twilight's kiss, love's pure divine.

A Path to Forgotten Lands

Beyond the hills where shadows lie,
Ancient paths beneath the sky.
Whispers guide the wandering feet,
To lands where history and mystery meet.

Footsteps echo on the dusty trails,
Tales of heroes, lost in gales.
Ruins speak of a time gone by,
In silent tones, they softly sigh.

Fields of wildflowers, colors bright,
Guard secrets hidden from the light.
Each petal tells of love and pain,
In forgotten lands, nothing is in vain.

Through the mist, the past awakes,
Every memory, a ripple it makes.
Journey on with a heart so grand,
Along the path to forgotten lands.

Beyond the Veil of Familiar

In the twilight, shadows blend,
Unseen realms begin to send.
A call to venture, a call so clear,
Beyond the veil of what we hold dear.

Echoes of laughter, whispers of grace,
Another world, another place.
Eyes wide open, hearts aglow,
In the depths of night, let curiosity flow.

Mysteries linger in every glance,
Promising wonders, a whispered chance.
Step through the seams of the known and run,
To realms where reality and dreams are spun.

With courage as your guiding light,
Explore the shadows, embrace the night.
Beyond the veil, where secrets are pure,
Awaits a magic, forever to endure.

The Atlas of Longing

In the quiet maps we sketch,
The dreams are drawn in whispers.
Each line a thread of hope,
Leading to the heart's desire.

Through valleys wide and mountains high,
We seek the stars just out of reach.
Every moment we embrace,
A step toward what could be.

Wanderers in this endless space,
Guided by an unseen hand.
In the depths of silent nights,
Longing finds its rightful place.

With every heartbeat echoing,
The map unfolds in shades of night.
We chart this course of yearning,
In the atlas of desire's light.

Illuminations Beyond the Known

In twilight's gentle embrace,
Shadows dance with fading light.
What lies beyond is shrouded still,
Yet sparks ignite the curious mind.

Stars whisper tales of the past,
Guiding souls through endless night.
With every step into the dark,
The unknown calls us ever near.

Questions linger on the breeze,
Carried forth like drifting leaves.
With each breath, the world expands,
Illuminations spark the heart.

So take my hand, and let's explore,
The realms where shadows softly fade.
For in the whispers of the night,
New horizons come alive.

Unraveled Threads of the Journey

Each thread a story left behind,
Woven deep within the soul.
In patterns strange and beautiful,
We find the truth of who we are.

Moments stitched together tight,
Frayed edges speak of battles fought.
With every twist, a lesson learned,
Unraveled paths lead us to peace.

In the tapestry of time we weave,
Colors blend in perfect harmony.
What seems a knot may hold a tale,
Of journeys taken, hearts made whole.

Step by step, we trace the lines,
Embrace the tapestry of dreams.
For in the threads of each moment,
Our story's light forever gleams.

The Heart's Compass to What Lies Ahead

In the depths of silent yearning,
The heart's compass spins and turns.
Guided by a gentle longing,
Drawn to what the future holds.

Every choice, a path unearthed,
With courage hidden in each step.
Through storms and clear skies we wander,
A map etched in the soul's design.

Trust is the beacon that lights the way,
Navigating through uncharted seas.
With patience, we await the dawn,
The heart leads where dreams may rise.

So here we stand, with eyes wide open,
Ready for the journey ahead.
Together, we'll embrace the unknown,
As the heart's compass guides us true.

The Boundary of Forgotten Dreams

In the dusk where shadows lay,
Whispers of hope softly sway.
Memories dance on the edge of night,
Fading traces of lost light.

Silent echoes of what once was,
Hearts entwined without a cause.
Every sigh a silent plea,
To reclaim what's meant to be.

Through the mist where wishes tread,
Stories linger of words unsaid.
On the brink of dreams untold,
Fathoms deep, treasures of gold.

Yet in the twilight, they recede,
A longing heart left to plead.
Boundaries drawn by fears unseen,
In the land of what has been.

Echoing Steps Through Time

Footfalls deep in the ancient ground,
Lost in tunes of the past profound.
Each step a story, a tale to find,
Whispers crossing the fabric of time.

Echoes drift through the still of night,
Carried onward by fading light.
Ghostly paths where memories weave,
In the breath of all who believe.

Seams of history gently frayed,
Fragments of hopes that once conveyed.
A dance of time, a fleeting glance,
In every echo, a second chance.

Through the ages, the footsteps lead,
Binding the hearts that dare to heed.
In each echo, a lifeline cast,
Threads of future bound to the past.

Veils of the Uncharted

Glistening mists that shroud the dawn,
Secrets linger where dreams are drawn.
Through the veils that cover the light,
Curious minds seek hidden sight.

Paths that twist beyond the known,
Journey's hand in the seeds they've sown.
Beyond horizons yet to appear,
Veils of wonder hold many a fear.

In shadows deep, insights await,
Mysteries knock at the gates of fate.
Each layer peels with a tender heart,
From the stillness, new worlds depart.

Veils of the uncharted call,
Dare to rise, dare to fall.
Through the fog, the brave will stride,
Into the realms where dreams abide.

Pathways Through the Silent Night

Stars alight in the velvet dark,
Guiding hearts with a quiet spark.
Moonlit paths that softly gleam,
Woven threads of a timeless dream.

In the stillness, secrets dwell,
Stories whispered, ancient spell.
Navigating through shadows so bright,
Hearts remember the silent night.

Footsteps fall on the dewy ground,
In this calm, the lost are found.
Every breath a gentle sigh,
As the world drifts slowly by.

Through the silence, voices sing,
Hope ignites as the night takes wing.
Pathways lead where the heart ignites,
Into the magic of starry nights.

Where the Sky Meets the Earth

The horizon holds its breath,
Where blue and ground embrace,
Fields stretch wide beneath the sun,
A timeless, gentle space.

Clouds drift lazily above,
Casting shadows on the land,
The earth and sky in silent pact,
A beauty unplanned.

Mountains stand with arms stretched high,
Kissing the heavens so grand,
While rivers run with whispered songs,
Through valleys, they expand.

In this place where worlds collide,
Nature sings a vibrant tune,
Where the sky meets the earth's embrace,
Under the watchful moon.

Voices in the Whispering Wind

Softly speak the ancient trees,
In the rustle of the leaves,
Carrying tales of distant lands,
In every breath that heaves.

The wind remembers every soul,
It holds their laughter tight,
Through valleys deep and mountains tall,
It carries them to light.

Fingers brush against the air,
Feeling stories intertwined,
Voices echo like a song,
In whispers, they're defined.

Listen close, for secrets soar,
On gentle gusts that play,
The wind will tell you all it knows,
If you just dare to stay.

A Tapestry of Faraway Echoes

Across the miles where shadows dwell,
A tapestry unfolds,
Weaving threads of ancient dreams,
In hues of blues and golds.

Echoes of a distant laugh,
Resound through time and space,
Each note a stitch in memory,
In this vast, sacred place.

Stories dance on every breeze,
Carried from afar,
A symphony of glowing nights,
Beneath a thousand stars.

Through this tapestry we roam,
Boundless, free, and bold,
In the echoes of the past,
The future's thread is told.

The Lure of Faded Memories

In dusty halls where silence sleeps,
Faded moments softly call,
Each photograph a secret kept,
Within the shadows' thrall.

Whispers of forgotten days,
Like echoes through the years,
The heart holds onto fleeting dreams,
In joys and silent fears.

Time's gentle hand can wear away,
The edges of the past,
Yet in the quiet of the night,
The memories hold fast.

The lure of dreams long gone away,
Draws us back to see,
Each heartbeat like a fleeting song,
A glimpse of what could be.

Dreams of Far-Off Realms

In twilight's glow, the wanderers roam,
Chasing whispers of a distant home.
Stars align in a mystical dance,
Guiding hearts through a fleeting chance.

Mountains rise where shadows play,
Casting dreams when night holds sway.
Across the winds, their tales unfold,
Of brave adventures, golden and bold.

Oceans whisper to sailors lost,
Echoing legends of greatness tossed.
In every wave, a story lies,
Of loves and battles beneath the skies.

So dream away in realms untold,
Where wonders bloom, and hearts are bold.
Listen closely to the calls of night,
For in your dreams, you'll find your light.

In the Quiet of the Unknown

In shadows deep, where silence dwells,
The secrets hide, like whispered bells.
Echoes of thoughts drift soft and low,
In stillness, truths begin to grow.

A fog encases the path ahead,
Each step uncertain, each word unsaid.
Yet in the calm, where time stands still,
Lies a beauty that words can't spill.

Wonders emerge from the depths of night,
Glimmers of hope, a fleeting light.
With gentle hands, we mold our fate,
In the quiet, we learn to wait.

Though darkness looms and fears may creep,
In the unknown, our souls shall leap.
For every shadow that dances near,
Holds the whispers that we long to hear.

Secrets Beyond the Walled World

Behind the stones, the stories hide,
Echoes of lives once lived inside.
With every crack, a tale is spun,
Of battles fought and victories won.

The ivy climbs with gentle grace,
Veiling time in a warm embrace.
In hidden nooks, the heartbeats blend,
Of lovers lost and dreams that mend.

Here lies a world both vast and small,
With laughter's echo and sorrow's call.
Past the barriers of stone and steel,
Are whispers that the night can heal.

Unlock the gates, let the light pour in,
Embrace the shadows where stories begin.
In every corner, a memory gleams,
In those secrets, we find our dreams.

Navigating the Celestial Divide

Stars scatter like seeds in the night,
Each one a beacon, a distant light.
Between the realms where shadows play,
We journey forth, come what may.

The moon provides a silvery guide,
As we traverse the cosmic tide.
With open hearts, we sail the skies,
Unveiling truths through ancient eyes.

Galaxies whisper of paths unknown,
In the vastness, we are never alone.
Our dreams emerge from the nebulae,
Chasing wonders that leap and fly.

So reach for stars, let your spirit soar,
For beyond the divide lies so much more.
In navigating the night's embrace,
We find our place in the endless space.

Beyond the Whispering Pines

Beneath the boughs where shadows play,
The secrets breathe in muted sway.
The gusts of wind, they softly call,
Inviting hearts to heed their thrall.

In twilight's glow, the branches sway,
As dreams drift softly, far away.
Each rustle sings of stories old,
In every sigh, a tale unfolds.

The moonlight weaves through emerald halls,
Where time unwinds and silence falls.
With every step, a memory gleams,
Among the whispers, lost in dreams.

Beyond the pines, the world awakes,
In nature's arms, our spirit shakes.
A path unknown, we dare to tread,
In harmony with what has said.

The Embrace of Faraway Lands

In distant shores where sunsets glow,
The ocean's breath whispers low.
With open arms, horizons meet,
As wanderers find their heart's retreat.

The mountains rise in shades of blue,
With clouds that drift like dreams anew.
Each valley cradles voices sweet,
In every corner, life's heartbeat.

Through bustling streets and quiet trails,
The spirit roams where wonder sails.
In every stone and every sound,
The beauty of this world is found.

Embraced by lands so far away,
We chase the dawn of each new day.
In unity with earth and sky,
Our souls entwined, we learn to fly.

Forgotten Roads and Wandering Souls

On pathways lost to time's own hand,
Where echoes dwell in shifting sand.
The wayward steps of those who've roamed,
Resonate within these bones.

Each faded sign tells tales of yore,
Of hearts that sought and hearts that bore.
With every stride, the stories blend,
In whispers, rhythms they transcend.

The roads we tread may lead us far,
Beneath the watchful evening star.
In solitude, we find our guide,
Embrace the night, let grace decide.

Wandering souls, our fates entwined,
Through winding paths, we seek to find.
In every mile, a piece of home,
Forever free, forever roam.

Chronicles of Forgotten Bridges

Across the water, silence sprawls,
Where time has built its gentle walls.
These bridges span the tales untold,
Of hearts once brave, of lives behold.

With every plank, a story sleeps,
In shadows deep, the memory keeps.
The whispers of the past still linger,
As curious hands trace each finger.

In twilight hues, their beauty shines,
In every crack, a thread of lines.
Connecting worlds of lost debut,
In dreams they weave, they welcome you.

The chronicles speak of love and fate,
Of journeys new and paths innate.
So step upon this aged span,
And journey forth, dear heart, you can.

Milton Keynes UK
Ingram Content Group UK Ltd.
UKHW022144111124
451073UK00007B/181